质量发展纲要

（2011—2020年）

Quality Development Outline

（2011-2020）

（汉英版）

中国质检出版社

China Zhijian Publishing House

图书在版编目(CIP)数据

质量发展纲要(2011—2020年)=Quality Development Outline(2011—2020):汉、英/《质量发展纲要(2011—2020年)》起草工作小组编著. —北京:中国质检出版社,2012(2012.3重印)
ISBN 978-7-5026-3550-3

Ⅰ.①质… Ⅱ.①质… Ⅲ.①质量管理—发展战略—中国—2011～2020—汉、英 Ⅳ.①F279.23

中国版本图书馆CIP数据核字(2012)第026155号

中国质检出版社出版发行
北京市朝阳区和平里西街甲2号(100013)
北京市西城区三里河北街16号(100045)

网址 www.spc.net.cn
总编室:(010)64275323 发行中心:(010)51780235
读者服务部:(010)68523946

中国标准出版社秦皇岛印刷厂印刷
各地新华书店经销

*

开本 880×1230 1/32 印张 3.125 字数 68 千字
2012年3月第一版 2012年3月第二次印刷

*

定价 12.00 元

目　　录

Contents

国务院关于印发质量发展纲要（2011—2020年）的通知

国发〔2012〕9号

各省、自治区、直辖市人民政府，国务院各部委、各直属机构：

现将《质量发展纲要（2011—2020年）》印发给你们，请认真贯彻执行。

国务院

二〇一二年二月六日

质量发展纲要

（2011—2020 年）

为深入贯彻落实科学发展观，促进经济发展方式转变，提高我国质量总体水平，实现经济社会又好又快发展，特制定本纲要。

一、质量发展的基础与环境

质量发展是兴国之道、强国之策。质量反映一个国家的综合实力，是企业和产业核心竞争力的体现，也是国家文明程度的体现；既是科技创新、资源配置、劳动者素质等因素的集成，又是法治环境、文化教育、诚信建设等方面的综合反映。质量问题是经济社会发展的战略问题，关系可持续发展，关系人民群众切身利益，关系国家形象。

党和国家历来高度重视质量工作。新中国成立尤其是改革开放以来，国家制定实施了一系列政策措施，初步形成了中国特色的质量发展之路。特别是国务院颁布实施《质量振兴纲要（1996 年—

2010年)》以来,全民质量意识不断提高,质量发展的社会环境逐步改善,我国主要产业整体素质和企业质量管理水平有较大提高,产品质量、工程质量、服务质量明显提升,原材料、基础元器件、重大装备、消费类及高新技术类产品的质量接近发达国家平均水平,一批国家重大工程质量达到国际先进水平,商贸、旅游、金融、物流等现代服务业服务质量明显改善,覆盖第一二三产业及社会事业领域的标准体系初步形成。但是,我国质量发展的基础还很薄弱,质量水平的提高仍然滞后于经济发展,片面追求发展速度和数量,忽视发展质量和效益的现象依然存在。产品、工程等质量问题造成的经济损失、环境污染和资源浪费仍然比较严重,质量安全特别是食品安全事故时有发生。一些生产经营者质量诚信缺失,肆意制售假冒伪劣产品,破坏市场秩序和社会公正,危害人民群众生命健康安全,损害国家信誉和形象。

新世纪的第二个十年,是我国全面建设小康社会、加快推进社会主义现代化的关键时期,是深化改革开放、加快转变经济发展方式的攻坚时期。在这一重要历史时期,经济全球化深入发展,科技进步日新月异,全球产业分工和市场需求结构出现明显变化，以质量为核心要素的标准、人才、技术、市场、资源等竞争日趋激烈。同时，我国工业化、信息化、城镇化、市场化、国际化进程加快，实现又好又快发展需要坚实的质量基础，满足人民群众日益增长的质量需求也对质量工作提出更高要求。面对新形势、新挑战，坚持以质取胜，建设质量强国，是保障和改善民生的迫切需要，是调整经济结构和转变发展方式的内在要求，是实现科学发展和全面建设小康社会的战略选择，是增强综合国力和实现中华民族伟大复兴的必由之路。

二、指导思想、工作方针和发展目标

（一）指导思想。高举中国特色社会主义伟大旗帜，以邓小平理论和“三个代表”重要思想为指导，深入贯彻落实科学发展观，从强化法治、落实责任、加强教育、增强全社会质量意识入手，立足当前，着眼长远，整体推进，突出重点，综合施策，标本兼治，全面提高质量管理水平，推动建设质量强国，促进经济社会又好又快发展。

（二）工作方针。以人为本，安全为先，诚信守法，夯实基础，创新驱动，以质取胜。

——把以人为本作为质量发展的价值导向。

质量发展必须不断满足人民群众日益增长的物质文化需要，更好地保障和改善民生。提高质量水平，促进质量发展，也必须依靠人民群众的共同努力。

——把安全为先作为质量发展的基本要求。强化质量安全意识，落实质量安全责任，严格质量安全监管，加强质量安全风险管理，提高质量安全保障能力，科学处置质量安全事件，切实保障广大人民群众的身体健康和生命财产安全。

——把诚信守法作为质量发展的重要基石。倡导诚实守信、合法经营。增强质量诚信意识，完善质量诚信体系，严厉打击质量违法行为，充分发挥市场机制作用，营造公平竞争、优胜劣汰的市场环境，发展先进的质量文化。

——把夯实基础作为质量发展的保障条件。深化理论研究，加强质量法治建设，夯实质量管理基础，加强质量人才培养，推进标准化、计量、认证认可以及检验检测能力建设，不断完善有利于质量发展的体制机制。

——把创新驱动作为质量发展的强大动力。加快技术进步，实现管理创新，提高劳动者素质，优化资源配置，增强创新能力，增强发展活力，推动质量事业全面、协调、可持续发展。

——把以质取胜作为质量发展的核心理念。坚持好字优先，好中求快。全面提高各行各业的质量管理水平，发挥质量的战略性、基础性和支撑性作用，依靠质量创造市场竞争优势，增强我国产品、企业、产业的核心竞争力。

（三）发展目标。到2020年，建设质量强国取得明显成效，质量基础进一步夯实，质量总体水平显著提升，质量发展成果惠及全体人民。形成一批拥有国际知名品牌和核心竞争力的优势企业，形成一批品牌形象突出、服务平台完备、质量水平一流的现代企业和产业集群，基本建成食品质量安全和重点产品质量检测体系，为全面建设小康社会和本世纪中叶基本实现社会主义现代化奠定坚实的质量基础。

1. 产品质量：到2020年，产品质量保障体系更加完善，产品质量安全指标全面达到国家强制性标准要求，质量创新能力和自有品牌市场竞争力明显提高，品种、质量、效益显著改善，节能环保性能大幅提升，基本满足人民群众日益增长的质量需求。农产品和食品实现优质、生态、安全，制造业主要行业和战略性新兴产业的产品质量水平达到或接近国际先进水平。

到 2015 年，产品质量发展的具体目标：

——农产品和食品质量安全水平稳定提高。农业标准化生产普及率超过 30%，主要农产品质量安全抽检合格率稳定在 96%以上。重点食品质量安全状况保持稳定良好。农产品和食品质量安全得到有效保障。

——制造业产品质量水平显著提升。产品质量合格率稳步提高，其中产品质量国家监督抽查合格率稳定在 90%以上，主要工业产品的质量损失率逐步下降，质量竞争力逐步提高，重大装备部分关键零部件、基础元器件、基础材料等重点工业产品和重要消费类产品的技术质量指标达到或接近国际先进水平。培育一批具有国际竞争力的自有品牌，品牌价值和效益明显提升。

——战略性新兴产业发展能力大幅提升。形成一批由我主导的国际标准，主要产品质量处于国际先进水平，培育一批质量素质高、品牌影响力大和核心竞争力强的大企业和一批创新活力旺盛的中小企业，推动战略性新兴产业发展成为先导性、支柱性产业。

2. 工程质量：到 2020 年，建设工程质量水平全面提升，国家重点工程质量达到国际先进水平，人民群众对工程质量满意度显著提高。

到2015年，工程质量发展的具体目标：

——工程质量水平显著提升。工程质量整体水平保持稳中有升，建筑、交通运输、水利电力等重大建设工程的耐久性、安全性普遍增强，工程质量通病治理取得显著成效，大中型工程项目一次验收合格率达到100%，其他工程一次验收合格率达到98%以上。人民群众对工程质量（尤其住宅质量）满意度明显提高，建设工程质量投诉率逐年下降。

——工程质量技术创新能力明显增强。在建筑、交通基础设施、清洁能源和新能源等重要工程领域拥有一批核心技术，节能、环保、安全、信息技术含量显著增加。建筑工程节能效率和工业化建造比重不断提高。绿色建筑发展迅速，住宅性能改善明显。

3. 服务质量：到2020年，全面实现服务质量的标准化、规范化和品牌化，服务业质量水平显著提升，建成一批国家级综合服务业标准化试点，骨干服务企业和重点服务项目的服务质量达到或接近国际先进水平，服务业品牌价值和效益大幅提升，推动实现服务业大发展。

到2015年，服务业质量发展的具体目标：

——生产性服务业质量全面提升。在金融服务、现代物流、高技术服务、商务服务、交通运输和信息服务等重点生产性服务领域，建立健全服务标准体系，全面实施服务质量国家标准。重点提升外包服务、研发设计、检验检测、售后服务、信用评价、品牌价值评价、认证认可等专业服务质量，促进生产性服务业与先进制造业融合。培育形成一批品牌影响力大、质量竞争力强的大型服务企业（集团）。生产性服务业顾客满意度达到80以上。

——生活性服务业质量显著改善。批发、零售、住宿、餐饮、居民服务、旅游、家庭服务、文化体育产业等生活性服务领域质量标准与国际先进水平接轨，标准覆盖率大幅提升，建成一批国家级服务标准化示范区。培育形成一批凝聚民族文化特色的服务品牌和精品服务项目，基本形成专业化、品牌化、网络化经营模式，服务产品种类不断丰富，满足人民群众多样化需求。行业自律能力和质量诚信意识明显增强，生活性服务业顾客满意度达到75以上。

专栏 1　质量发展主要指标	
01	产品质量(2015 年) 农业标准化生产普及率超过 30% 主要农产品质量安全抽检合格率稳定在 96%以上 产品质量国家监督抽查合格率稳定在 90%以上
02	工程质量(2015 年) 大中型工程项目一次验收合格率达到 100% 其他工程一次验收合格率达到 98%以上
03	服务质量(2015 年) 生产性服务业顾客满意度达到 80 以上 生活性服务业顾客满意度达到 75 以上

三、强化企业质量主体作用

(一) 严格企业质量主体责任。建立企业质量安全控制关键岗位责任制，明确企业法定代表人或主要负责人对质量安全负首要责任、企业质量主管人员对质量安全负直接责任。严格实施企业岗位质量规范与质量考核制度，实行质量安全“一票否决”。企业要严格执行重大质量事故报告及应急处理制度，健全产品质量追溯体系，切实履行质量担保责任及缺陷产品召回等法定义务，依法承担质量损害赔偿责任。

(二) 提高企业质量管理水平。企业要建立健全质量管理体系，加强全员、全过程、全方位的质量管理，严格按标准组织生产经营，严格质量控制，严格质量检验和计量检测。大力推广先进技术手段和现代质量管理理念方法，广泛开展质量改进、质量攻关、质量比对、质量风险分析、质量成本控制、质量管理小组等活动。积极应用减量化、资源化、再循环、再利用、再制造等绿色环保技术，大力发展低碳、清洁、高效的生产经营模式。

（三）加快企业质量技术创新。把技术创新作为企业提高质量的抓手，切实加大技术创新投入，加快科技成果转化，注重创新成果的标准化和专利化，扭转重制造轻研发、重引进轻消化、重模仿轻创新的状况。积极应用新技术、新工艺、新材料，改善品种质量，提升产品档次和服务水平，研究开发具有核心竞争力、高附加值和自主知识产权的创新性产品和服务。鼓励有条件的企业建立技术中心、工程中心、产业化基地，努力培育集研发、设计、制造和系统集成于一体的创新型企业。

（四）发挥优势企业引领作用。努力推动中央企业和行业骨干企业成为国际标准的主要参与者和国家标准、行业标准的实施主体，将质量管理的成功经验和先进方法向产业链两端延伸推广，带动提升整体质量水平。发挥优势企业对中小企业的带动提升作用，鼓励制定企业联盟标准，引领新产品开发和品牌创建，带动中小企业实施技术改造升级和管理创新，提升专业化分工协作水平和市场服务能力，增强质量竞争力。

（五）推动企业履行社会责任。强化以确保质量安全、促进可持续发展为基本要求的企业社会责任理念，建立健全履行社会责任的机制，将履行社会责任融入企业经营管理决策。推动企业积极承担对员工、消费者、投资者、合作方、社区和环境等利益相关方的社会责任。鼓励企业发布社会责任报告，强化诚信自律，践行质量承诺，在经济、环境和社会方面创造综合价值，树立对社会负责的良好形象。

四、加强质量监督管理

（一）加快质量法治建设。牢固树立质量法治理念，坚持运用法律手段解决质量发展中的突出矛盾和问题。健全质量法律法规，研究制定完善质量安全和质量责任追究等法律法规。严格依法行政，规范执法行为，保证严格执法、公正执法、文明执法。加强执法队伍建设，开展对执法人员的培养与培训，提高执法人员综合素质和执法水平。完善质量法制监督机制，落实执法责任，切实做到有权必有责、用权受监督、侵权须赔偿、违法要追究。加强质量法制宣传教育，普及质量法律知识，营造学法、用法、守法的良好社会氛围。

（二）强化质量安全监管。制定实施国家重点监管产品目录，加强对关系国计民生、健康安全、节能环保的重点产品、重大设备、重点工程及重点服务项目的监管。加强对食品、药品、妇女儿童老人用品以及农业生产资料、建筑材料、重要消费品、应急物资的监督检查，完善生产许可、强制性产品认证、重大设备监理、进出口商品法定检验、特种设备安全监察、登记管理等监管制度。强化城乡结合部和农村市场等重点区域，以及生产、流通、进出口环节质量安全监管，增强产品质量安全溯源能力，建立质量安全联系点制度，健全质量安全监管长效机制。

（三）实施质量安全风险管理。建立企业重大质量事故报告制度和产品伤害监测制度，加强对重点产品、重点行业和重点地区的质量安全风险监测和分析评估，对区域性、行业性、系统性质量风险及时预警，对重大质量安全隐患及时提出处置措施。建立和完善动植物外来有害生物防御体系、进出口农产品和食品质量安全保障体系、进出口工业品质量安全监控体系和国境卫生检疫风险监控体系，有效降低动植物疫情疫病传入传出风险，保障进出口农产品、食品和工业品质量安全，防止传染病跨境传播。完善质量安全风险管理工作机制，制定质量安全风险应急预案，加强风险信息资源共享，提升风险防范和应急处置能力，切实做到对质量安全风险的早发现、早研判、早预警、早处置。

专栏 2　建立健全质量安全风险管理体系	
01	强化食品质量安全风险预警 组织实施集中、高效、针对性强的食品安全风险预警，完善食品安全信息收集、风险监测、预警通报等功能。重点加强食品安全风险监测网络建设，强化非法添加物和食品添加剂监测，及时开展安全评估，切实防范系统性风险。
02	完善产品伤害监测系统 质检、卫生等部门共同建立产品伤害监测系统，收集、统计、分析与产品相关的伤害信息，评估产品安全的潜在风险，及时发出产品伤害预警，为政府部门、行业组织及企业等制定防范措施提供依据。

专栏2　建立健全质量安全风险管理体系	
03	加强产品质量安全风险预警 搭建产品质量安全信息收集网络，建立产品质量安全信息舆情监控系统，完善产品质量安全风险预警公共技术服务，加强高危行业、重点产品及进出口商品的质量安全风险监测，提升产品质量安全风险评估和预警效能。
04	健全进出境动植物检疫和国境卫生检疫疫情风险监控 完善进出境动植物检疫和国境卫生检疫疫情风险信息收集网络，做好进出境动植物检疫标准法规、风险监测、风险评估、风险预警、疫情信息、检疫截获信息等公共技术和信息服务，增强口岸卫生检疫和动植物检疫能力。

（四）加强宏观质量统计分析。建立健全以产品质量合格率、出口商品质量合格率、顾客满意指数以及质量损失率等为主要内容的质量指标体系，推动质量指标纳入国民经济和社会发展统计指标体系。各地方、各行业要结合实际情况，建立和完善质量状况分析报告制度，定期评估分析质量状况及质量竞争力水平，比较研究国内外质量发展趋势，为宏观经济决策提供依据。

（五）推进质量诚信体系建设。健全质量信用信息收集与发布制度。搭建以组织机构代码实名制为基础、以物品编码管理为溯源手段的质量信用信息平台，推动行业质量信用建设，实现银行、商务、海关、税务、工商、质检、工业、农业、保险、统计等多部门质量信用信息互通与共享。完善企业质量信用档案和产品质量信用信息记录，健全质量信用评价体系，实施质量信用分类监管。建立质量失信“黑名单”并向社会公开，加大对质量失信惩戒力度。鼓励发展质量信用服务机构，规范发展质量信用评价机构，促进质量信用产品的推广使用，建立多层次、全方位的质量信用服务市场。

（六）依法严厉打击质量违法行为。加大生产源头治理力度，强化市场监督管理，深入开展重点产品、重点工程、重点行业、重点地区和重点市场质量执法，严厉查办制假售假大案要案，严厉打击危害公共安全、人身健康以及生命财产安全等质量违法行为，严厉查办利用高科技手段从事质量违法活动。加强执法协作，建立健全处置重大质量违法突发案件快速反应机制和执法联动机制，加强行业性、区域性产品质量问题集中整治，深入开展农业生产资料、建筑材料等产品打假，保护广大人民群众的合法权益。建立健全质量安全有奖举报制度，切实落实对举报人的奖励，保护举报人的合法权益。做好行政执法与刑事司法的有效衔接，加大质量违法行为的刑事司法打击力度。

五、创新质量发展机制

（一）完善质量工作体制机制。完善符合社会主义市场经济发展要求、具有中国特色的质量宏观管理体制。健全地方政府负总责、监管部门各负其责、企业是第一责任人的质量安全责任体系。构建政府监管、市场调节、企业主体、行业自律、社会参与的质量工作格局，充分运用经济、法律、行政等手段维护质量安全，充分发挥市场和企业在促进质量发展中的能动作用。加大政府质量综合管理和质量安全保障能力投入，合理配置行政资源，强化质量工作基础建设，提升质量监管部门的履职能力，逐步在经济技术开发区、高新技术产业园区等功能区以及产业集中的乡镇建立质量监管和技术服务机构。广泛开展质量强省（区、市）活动，形成全社会齐抓共管的良好氛围。

（二）健全质量评价考核机制。建立健全科学规范的质量工作绩效考核评价体系，完善地方各级人民政府和有关行业质量工作的评价指标和考核制度，将质量安全和质量发展纳入地方各级人民政府绩效考核评价内容。加强考核结果的反馈，强化考核结果运用，绩效考核结果作为领导班子和领导干部综合考核评价的内容，作为领导班子建设和领导干部选拔任用、培养教育、管理监督、激励约束的依据。严格质量事故调查和责任追究，加大警示问责和督导整改力度，严肃查处质量事故涉及的渎职腐败行为。

（三）强化质量准入退出机制。发挥质量监管职能作用，对高污染、高耗能、高排放及资源浪费的行业和产品，严格市场准入，加快淘汰落后产能，促进结构优化升级。对涉及人身健康、财产安全的产品和重要敏感进出口商品，进一步严格质量准入条件，提高市场准入门槛。建立健全缺陷产品和不安全食品召回制度。对不能满足准入条件、不能保证质量安全和整改后仍然达不到要求的企业，依法强制退出。对存在严重违法行为的，坚决依法取缔。

（四）创新质量发展激励机制。建立国家和地方质量奖励制度，对质量管理先进、成绩显著的组织和个人给予表彰奖励，树立先进典型，激励广大企业和全社会重质量、讲诚信、树品牌。通过国家中小企业发展专项资金，支持中小企业产品研发、质量攻关。鼓励企业积极开展争创质量管理先进班组和质量标兵活动，鼓励质量工作者争创“五一”劳动奖。

（五）创建品牌培育激励机制。大力实施名牌发展战略，发挥品牌引领作用，制定并实施培育品牌发展的制度措施，开展知名品牌创建工作。加大自主知识产权产品的保护力度，建设有利于品牌发展的长效机制和良好环境。支持企业依托技术标准开拓海外市场，实施品牌经营和市场多元化战略，打造世界知名品牌。建立品牌建设国家标准体系和品牌价值评价制度，完善与国际接轨的品牌价值评价体系，增强品牌价值评价国际话语权。进一步加强地理标志产品、中国驰名商标及地方名牌产品等工作。

专栏3　品牌建设重点措施	
01	建立品牌建设标准体系 围绕质量核心，加强品牌培育、品牌管理和品牌评价方法研究，制定品牌的术语、要素、评价要求和建设指南等国家标准，建立符合中国国情、与国际接轨的品牌建设国家标准体系。

专栏 3　品牌建设重点措施	
02	建立品牌价值评价制度 　　以消费者认可、市场竞争中产生为原则，参照国际标准和国际惯例，以品牌货币价值评价为主要内容，以装备制造、钢铁有色、纺织服装、轻工家电、电子信息、汽车制造、石油化工、现代物流、旅游等优势产业为重点，建立具有中国特色的品牌价值评价体系和制度，提高中国品牌的国际化水平。
03	开展知名品牌创建工作 　　制定创建条件和配套政策措施，以产业聚集区、国家自主创新示范区、经济技术开发区、高新技术产业园区、现代服务区、旅游景区等为重点，推动地方人民政府开展知名品牌创建工作，规范产业发展，扩大品牌影响，提升区域经济竞争力。

（六）建立质量安全多元救济机制。积极探索实施符合市场经济规则、有利于消费者维权的产品质量安全多元救济机制。完善产品侵权责任制度，建立产品质量安全责任保险制度，保障质量安全事故受害者得到合理、及时的补偿。引导企业、行业协会、保险以及评估机构加强合作，降低质量安全风险，切实维护企业和消费者合法权益。

六、优化质量发展环境

（一）加强质量文化建设。牢固树立质量是企业生命的理念，实施以质取胜的经营战略。将诚实守信、持续改进、创新发展、追求卓越的质量精神转化为社会、广大企业及企业员工的行为准则，自觉抵制违法生产经营行为。推进社会主义先进质量文化建设，提升全民质量意识，倡导科学理性、优质安全、节能环保的消费理念，努力形成政府重视质量、企业追求质量、社会崇尚质量、人人关心质量的良好氛围，提升质量文化软实力。

（二）营造良好市场环境。建立各类企业依法使用生产要素、公平参与市场竞争、平等受到法律保护的环境。把优质安全作为扩大市场需求的积极要素，进一步释放城乡居民消费潜力，促进社会资源向优质产品、优秀品牌和优势企业聚集。打击垄断经营和不正当竞争，坚决破除地方保护，维护市场秩序，形成公平有序、优胜劣汰的市场环境。引导企业参与国际合作与交流，树立我国企业、产品良好国际形象，提升国际竞争力。

（三）完善质量投诉和消费维权机制。健全质量投诉处理机构，运用现代信息技术完善质量投诉信息平台，充分发挥 12365、12315 等投诉热线的作用，畅通质量投诉和消费维权渠道。积极推进质量仲裁检验和质量鉴定，有效调解和处理质量纠纷，化解社会矛盾。增强公众的质量维权意识，建立社会质量监督员制度。支持和鼓励消费者依法开展质量维权活动，更好地维护用户和消费者权益。

（四）发挥社会中介服务作用。加强质量管理、检验检测、计量校准、合格评定、信用评价等社会中介组织建设，推动质量服务的市场化进程。加强对质量服务市场的监管与指导，鼓励整合重组，推进质量服务机构规模化、网络化和品牌化建设，培育我国质量服务品牌。行业协会、学会、商会等社会团体要积极提供技术、标准、质量管理、品牌建设等方面的咨询服务，及时反映企业及消费者的质量需求，依据市场规则建立自律性运行机制，进一步促进行业规范发展，充分发挥中介组织在质量发展中的桥梁纽带作用。

（五）加强质量舆论宣传。深入开展全国“质量月”、“3·15”国际消费者权益保护日等形式多样、内容丰富的群众性质量活动，深入企业、机关、社区、乡村普及质量基础知识。坚持正确的舆论导向，大力宣传质量工作方针政策、法律法规以及质量管理先进典型。加强质量舆论监督，加大对质量违法案件的曝光力度，震慑质量违法行为。充分发挥新闻媒体质量舆论宣传的主渠道作用，引导各类媒体客观发布质量问题信息。

（六）深化质量国际交流合作。积极参加和主办国际质量大会，交流质量管理和技术成果，开展务实合作。围绕国家重大产业、区域经济发展规划及检验检测技术、标准一致性，建立双边、多边质量合作磋商机制，参与质量相关国际和区域性标准、规则制定，促进我国标准、计量、认证认可体系与国际接轨。积极应对国外技术性贸易措施，完善我国技术性贸易措施体系。鼓励国内企业、科研院所、大专院校、社会团体开展国际质量交流与合作，引进国外先进质量管理方法、技术和高端人才。

七、夯实质量发展基础

（一）推进质量创新能力建设。加大质量科技投入，加强质量研究机构和质量教育学科建设，形成分层级的质量人才培养格局，培育一批质量科技领军人才，探索建立具有中国特色的质量管理理论、方法和技术体系，加大质量科技成果转化应用力度。加快建立以企业为主体、市场为导向、产学研相结合的质量技术创新体系，发挥优势企业、重点科研院所和高等院校创新要素集聚的优势，建立一批重点突出、优势互补、资源共享的质量创新基地。推动实施重大质量改进和技术改造项目，培育形成以技术、标准、品牌、服务为核心的质量新优势。

（二）加强标准化工作。加快现代农业、先进制造业、战略性新兴产业、现代服务业、节能减排、社会管理和公共服务等领域国家标准体系建设。实施标准分类管理，加强强制性标准管理。缩短标准制修订周期，提升标准的先进性、有效性和适用性。积极采用国际标准，增强实质性参与国际标准化活动的能力，推动我国优势技术与标准成为国际标准，积极参与制修订影响我国相关产业发展的国际标准，提高应对全球技术标准竞争的能力。完善标准化管理体制，创新标准化工作机制，加强标准化与科技、经济和社会发展政策的有效衔接，促进军民标准化工作的有效融合。构建标准化科技支撑体系和公共服务体系，健全国家技术标准资源服务平台。

专栏4　标准化工作重点	
01	现代农业 　　完善农业物资条件、基础设施、生产技术、产品质量、运输存储、市场贸易以及农产品质量检测、动植物疫病防控以及农业社会化服务等农业标准体系，研究制定支撑高产、优质、高效、生态、安全农产品生产的技术标准。
02	战略性新兴产业 　　制定战略性新兴产业的标准化建设规划，加快建立有利于战略性新兴产业发展的标准体系，开展战略性新兴产业标准制定的示范试点工作。
03	现代服务业 　　积极拓展服务业标准化工作领域，建立完善细化、深化生产性服务业分工的质量标准与行业规范，进一步制定完善生活性服务业标准，建立健全重点突出、结构合理、科学适用的服务质量国家标准体系，重要服务行业和关键服务领域实现标准全覆盖，扩大服务标准覆盖范围。
04	节能减排领域 　　建立和完善资源、能源与环境标准体系，重点研制推动资源节约的先进技术标准、领跑者能效标准、高耗能产品能耗限额标准、终端用能产品能效标准、交通工具燃料消耗量限值标准、取水定额标准、废旧产品回收利用与再生资源标准，完善资源节约标准体系。
05	社会管理领域 　　建立健全教育、卫生、人口、公共就业和人才服务、劳动关系、社会保险、社会管理等社会事业领域的标准化体系，促进社会公平正义，推动和谐社会建设。
06	标准化示范、试点项目 　　在农业、服务业、循环经济、高新技术、国家重大工程等领域培育一批国家级标准化示范区和示范试点项目。

（三）强化计量基础支撑作用。紧密结合新型工业化进程，建立并完善以量子物理为基础，具有高精确度、高稳定性和与国际一致性的计量基标准以及量值传递和测量溯源体系。紧跟国际前沿计量科技发展趋势，针对国家战略性新兴产业发展、节能减排、循环经济、贸易公平、改善民生等计量新需求，加强计量标准体系建设，大力推进法制计量，全面加强工业计量，积极拓展工程计量，强化能源计量监管，培育和规范计量校准市场，加强计量检测技术的研究应用。提升计量服务能力，建设一批重大精密测量基础设施，建立完善国家计量科技创新基地和共享服务平台。尽快形成适应经济社会发展的计量体系。

（四）推动完善认证认可体系。参照国际通行规则，建立健全法律规范、行政监管、认可约束、行业自律、社会监督相结合的认证认可管理模式，完善认证认可体系，提升认证认可服务能力，提高强制性产品认证的有效性，推动自愿性产品认证健康有序发展，完善管理体系和服务认证制度。进一步培育和规范认证、检测市场，加强对认证机构、实验室和检查机构的监督管理。稳步推进国际互认，提高认证认可国际规则制定的参与度和话语权，提升中国认证认可国际影响力。

专栏5　认证认可工作重点	
01	提升认可能力 研究开发新型认可制度，推进食品安全领域良好农业规范(GAP)、危害分析和关键控制点(HACCP)、节能减排等认可工作。保持实验室认可数量和能力稳步增长。
02	完善强制性产品认证 开展强制性产品认证质量状况分析、安全风险评估和公共质量安全评价，加强对从业机构和人员、获证企业及产品的监督检查，健全强制性产品认证质量可追溯体系，促进认证产品质量水平全面提高。
03	推动自愿性产品认证 完善国家自愿性认证制度。强化节能、节水、节电、节油、可再生资源和环境标志产品认证，推动环保装备和综合利用装备产品认证。加强对有机产品、绿色食品、无公害农产品等认证有效性的监管。
04	提升管理体系认证水平 深化质量、环境、职业健康安全管理体系认证，努力提高认证有效性，积极拓展认证领域，推动管理体系标准在社会管理、文化教育医疗及新兴产业的广泛应用。加强信息技术服务、供应链安全体系认证的技术研发。
05	完善信息安全认证认可体系 加强信息安全认证认可制度和能力建设，健全信息安全认证认可工作体系，促进信息安全认证认可结果的社会采信。
06	加快实施服务认证 加快新型服务认证制度研发及实施进度，推进交通运输业、金融服务业、信息服务业、商务服务业、旅游业、体育产业等重点领域认证认可制度的建立和实施。

（五）加快检验检测技术保障体系建设。推进技术机构资源整合，优化检验检测资源配置，建设检测资源共享平台，完善食品、农产品质量快速检验检测手段，提高检验检测能力。加强政府实验室和检测机构建设，对涉及国计民生的产品质量安全实施有效监督。建立健全科学、公正、权威的第三方检验检测体系，鼓励不同所有制形式的技术机构平等参与市场竞争。对技术机构进行分类指导和监管，规范检验检测行为，促进技术机构完善内部管理和激励机制，提高检验检测质量和服务水平，提升社会公信力。支持技术机构实施“走出去”战略，创建国际一流技术机构。

专栏6　提升检验检测能力	
01	检测仪器装备研发 加大检验检测技术和检测装备的研发力度，推进重点仪器、关键检测设备的国产化进程，加快快速检测仪器设备、方法的筛选、推广和应用。
02	检测机构建设 推进实验室国际互认，建设一批高水平的国家产品质量监督检验中心、重点实验室和型式评价实验室，形成专业齐全、布局合理的地方和区域中心实验室格局。
03	检测资源共享平台建设 加强产业聚集地区公共检验检测技术服务平台建设，提高对中小企业检测的便利化服务能力。

专栏 6　提升检验检测能力	
04	检验检疫能力建设 增强技术性贸易措施应对和实施能力，加强出入境疫病疫情监控和进出口商品检验技术能力建设。在经济技术开发区、高新技术产业园区和出口加工区，建设一批面向设计开发、生产制造、售后服务全过程的公共检测技术服务平台。构建一批具有自主品牌的专业实验室检测联盟。
05	重点专项 开展提升食品质量安全检测和风险监测能力专项建设、重点产业产品和工程质量检测体系专项建设。

（六）推进质量信息化建设。加快质量信息网络工程建设，运用物联网等信息化手段，依托物品编码和组织机构代码等国家基础信息资源，加强产品质量和工程质量信息的采集、追踪、分析和处理，提高质量控制和质量管理的信息化水平，提升质量安全动态监管、质量风险预警、突发事件应对、质量信用管理的效能。推动信息化与工业化深度融合，提高产品质量和工程质量信息化水平。

八、实施质量提升工程

（一）质量素质提升工程。通过质量知识普及教育、职业教育和专业人才培养等措施，提升全民质量素养。建立中小学质量教育社会实践基地，普及质量知识。鼓励有条件的高等学校设立质量管理相关专业，培养质量专业人才。建立和规范各类质量教育培训机构，广泛开展面向企业的质量教育培训，重点加强对企业经营者的质量管理培训，加强对一线工人的工艺规程和操作技术培训，提高企业全员质量意识和质量技能。到2015年，基本完善国家质量专业技术人员职业资格以及注册设备监理师、注册计量师等制度。

（二）可靠性提升工程。在汽车、机床、航空航天、船舶、轨道交通、发电设备、工程机械、特种设备、家用电器、元器件和基础件等重点行业实施可靠性提升工程。加强产品可靠性设计、试验及生产过程质量控制，依靠技术进步、管理创新和标准完善，提升可靠性水平，促进我国产品质量由符合性向适用性、高可靠性转型。到2020年，我国基础件、通用件及关键自动化测控部件等可靠性水平满足国内市场需求，重点产品的可靠性达到或接近国际先进水平。百万千瓦级核电设备、新能源发电设备、高速动车组、高档数控机床与基础制造装备等一批重大装备可靠性达到国际先进水平。

（三）服务质量满意度提升工程。根据生产性和生活性服务业的不同特点，建立健全服务标准体系和服务质量测评体系，在交通运输、现代物流、银行保险、商贸流通、旅游住宿、医疗卫生、邮政通讯、社区服务等重点领域，建立顾客满意度评价制度，推进服务业满意度评价试点。引导企业提高服务质量，满足市场需求，促进服务市场标准化、规范化、国际化发展。

（四）质量对比提升工程。在农业、工业、建筑业和服务业等行业，分类分层次广泛开展质量对比提升活动。比照国际国内先进水平，在重点行业和支柱产业，开展竞争性绩效对比；在产业链和区域范围内，开展重点企业和产品的过程质量和管理绩效对比。制定质量对比提升工作制度，建立科学评价方法，完善质量对标分析数据库，为制定发展战略、明确发展目标提供质量改进的参考和依据。制定质量改进和赶超措施，优化生产工艺、更新生产设备、创新管理模式，改进市场销售战略。建立质量提升服务平台，完善对中小企业信息咨询、技术支持等公共服务和社会服务体系，实现质量提升和赶超。到 2015 年，在重要产业领域的 5 万家企业开展质量对比提升活动，使先进质量管理理念得到广泛传播，科学的质量管理方法和技术得到普遍采用，骨干和支柱行业内领先企业的质量达到国际先进水平。

（五）清洁生产促进工程。积极推进清洁生产模式。加快制修订与节能减排和循环经济有关的标准，建立健全低碳产品标识、能效标识、再生产品标识与低碳认证、节能产品认证等制度。落实和完善有利于清洁生产的财税政策。构建清洁生产技术服务平台，加快节能减排技术研发，攻克一批关键性技术难关。建立能源计量监测体系，加强对重点能耗企业能源计量监督管理。建立市场准入与退出机制，严格高耗能、高污染项目生产许可管理，加大淘汰落后产能力度。到 2015 年，清洁生产新技术产业化和标准化水平大幅提升，建成一批清洁生产示范项目和公共服务平台，生产过程污染物的产生和排放得到有效控制，资源消耗大幅降低。

九、组织实施

（一）加强组织领导。国务院质量主管部门应当根据工作需要组织召开联席会议，加强对质量工作的统筹规划和组织领导，制订落实本纲要的年度行动计划，研究解决和协调处理重大质量问题，督促检查本纲要贯彻实施情况。地方各级人民政府、各行业主管部门要按照纲要的部署和要求，把质量发展目标纳入本地区、本行业国民经济社会发展规划，加强质量政策引导，将质量工作列入重要议事日程，制定实施方案，明确目标责任，认真组织实施，切实提高质量发展的组织保障水平。

（二）完善配套政策。地方各级人民政府、各行业主管部门要围绕建设质量强国，制定本地区、本行业促进质量发展的相关配套政策和措施，加大对质量工作的投入，完善相关产业、环境、科技、金融、财税、人才培养等政策措施。在执行过程中加强本纲要与“十二五”国民经济和社会发展规划及其他有关规划的政策衔接，确保本纲要提出的各项目标得以实现。

（三）狠抓工作落实。地方各级人民政府、各行业主管部门要将落实质量发展的远期规划同解决当前突出的质量问题结合起来，使近期要求、实施步骤更有针对性，突出重点区域、重点领域、重点环节、重点产品和重点人群，有效解决事关公共安全、人身健康和生命财产安全的重点质量问题。各地方、各部门要联系本地区、本部门质量安全中的实际问题，落实本纲要及年度行动计划确定的发展目标和重点任务，夯实质量基础，保障质量安全，促进质量发展。

（四）强化检查考核。地方各级人民政府、各行业主管部门要建立落实本纲要的工作责任制，对纲要的实施情况进行严格检查考核，务求各项工作落到实处，确保质量发展取得实效。对纲要实施过程中取得突出成绩的单位和个人予以表彰奖励。国务院将适时检查考核本纲要的贯彻实施情况。

关于《质量发展纲要(2011—2020年)》的编制说明

国家质检总局

国家质检总局依据《"十二五"期间报国务院审批的专项规划整体预案的通知》要求，会同国家发展改革委等14个部门，编制了《质量发展纲要(2011—2020年)》(以下简称《纲要》)。

一、编制背景

质量问题是经济社会发展的一个战略问题。党和国家历来高度重视质量工作。新中国成立以来，尤其是改革开放以来，党中央、国务院制定实施了一系列政策措施，初步形成了中国特色的质量发展之路。以胡锦涛同志为总书记的党中央，对质量工作更加重视。党的十七大报告明确要求"以质取胜"，"确保产品质量和安全"，"实现速度和结构质量效益相统一"。温家宝总理在2007年的全国质量工作会议上强调，要坚持质量第一方针，全面提升我国产品质量水平。

1996年，国务院颁布实施《质量振兴纲要（1996年—2010年）》以来，全民质量意识不断增强，质量发展的社会环境逐步改善，主要产业整体素质和企业质量管理水平有了较大幅度提高，产品质量、工程质量、服务质量显著提升。其中，产品质量国家监督抽查合格率从1996年的75%提高到2010年的87.6%，出口商品的质量和档次稳步提高，质量竞争力逐步增强。一批国家重大工程质量达到国际先进水平。商贸、旅游、金融、物流等现代服务业服务质量有较大改善。覆盖第一二三产业及社会事业领域的标准体系初步形成，计量检测、认证认可及质量检验检测技术服务体系基本建立。各地质量兴（强）省、质量兴市（县）活动广泛开展，全社会重视质量的氛围初步形成。

但是，我国质量发展的基础还很薄弱，质量水平的提高仍然滞后于经济发展。片面追求发展速度和数量，忽视发展质量和效益的现象依然存在。由于产品、工程等质量问题造成的经济损失、环境污染、资源浪费比较严重。2011年产品质量国家监督抽查不合格率为12.5%，不合格产品的绝对数还很大。质量安全形势仍然严峻，产品质量安全特别是食品安全事故时有发生。一些生产经营者质量诚信缺失，肆意制售假冒伪劣产品，危害人民群众生命健康安全，损害国家信誉和形象。与发达国家相比，“中国制造”质量竞争力还不够强，缺少具有国际影响力的知名品牌和产品。质量问题已成为我国经济社会健康发展的一个制约因素。

新世纪的第二个十年，是我国全面建设小康社会、加快推进社会主义现代化的关键时期，是深化改革开放、加快转变经济发展方式的攻坚时期，也是质量发展的又一个重要时期。从国际上看，经济全球化深入发展，科技进步日新月异，全球产业分工和市场需求结构出现明显变化，以质量为核心要素的标准、人才、技术、市场、资源等竞争日趋激烈。从国内看，我国工业化、信息化、城镇化、市场化、国际化进程加快，要贯彻落实科学发展观，实现又好又快发展，需要坚实的质量基础；要加快转变经济发展方式，特别是实现制造业由大变强，需要可靠的质量支撑；要满足人民群众日益增长的质量需求也需要更强的质量保障能力。

《质量振兴纲要(1996 年—2010 年)》已经到期，制定新的质量纲要十分迫切。考虑与 2020 年实现全面建成小康社会的奋斗目标相呼应，质检总局报请国务院批准，专门组织编制2011年至2020年十年《质量发展纲要》，明确未来十年质量发展的总体目标、任务要求和政策措施，进一步动员全社会重视质量，增强质量意识，加强质量工作，提升质量水平，建设质量强国，为全面建设小康社会提供质量保障。

二、起草过程

《纲要》起草工作于2010年3月正式启动，质检总局会同发改委等14个部门专门成立了编制工作领导小组和起草工作小组，还成立了由中国工程院院士担任组长的编制工作专家咨询组。《纲要》起草过程中，搜集研究了大量国内外参考资料，并就涉及的重要制度和重大问题专门组织课题研究小组，开展广泛的社会调查和深入的理论研究工作。起草小组先后召开了16次起草工作会议、5次部门和行业论证会议、3次地方调研座谈会、2次中央企业座谈会以及2次专家咨询论证会，在此基础上集中撰稿，反复修改完善，形成《纲要》初稿。2011年6月9日，召开《纲要》专家论证会，来自质量管理、宏观经济、对外贸易、产业科技、法制研究等领域的22位专家一致同意《纲要》初稿。《纲要》报国务院后，国务院办公厅对《纲要》作了进一步修改完善，并再次征求了质检总局和其他14个会签部门以及中央组织部、教育部、监察部、财政部、人力资源和社会保障部、法制办等相关部门的意见。同时，还根据国务院领导同志对6位国务院参事提出的《关于建设质量强国的建议》的批示，对《纲要》作了补充完善，形成了《纲要》送审稿。

三、主要内容

《纲要》分为9个部分，提出了未来十年质量发展的指导思想、工作方针、发展目标、重点任务和政策措施。

第一部分质量发展的基础与环境。简要总结质量振兴取得的成效，梳理存在的问题，分析面临的形势。

第二部分指导思想、工作方针和发展目标。《纲要》明确了“高举中国特色社会主义伟大旗帜，以邓小平理论和‘三个代表’重要思想为指导，深入贯彻落实科学发展观，从强化法治、落实责任、加强教育、增强全社会质量意识入手，立足当前，着眼长远，整体推进，突出重点，综合施策，标本兼治，全面提高质量管理水平，推动建设质量强国，促进经济社会又好又快发展”的指导思想。提出了“以人为本，安全为先，诚信守法，夯实基础，创新驱动，以质取胜”的工作方针。制定了到 2015 年和 2020 年产品质量、工程质量、服务质量的发展目标。

第三部分强化企业质量主体作用。提出了 5 项要求，即：严格企业质量主体责任，提高企业质量管理水平，加快企业质量技术创新，发挥优势企业引领作用，推动企业履行社会责任。

第四部分加强质量监督管理。从政府的角度，提出了 6 项措施，即：加快质量法治建设，强化质量安全监管，实施质量安全风险管理，加强宏观质量统计分析，推进质量诚信体系建设和依法严厉打击质量违法行为。

第五部分创新质量发展机制。从质量创新发展的角度，提出了 6 个方面的内容，即：完善质量工作体制机制、健全质量评价考核机制、强化质量准入退出机制、创新质量发展激励机制、创建品牌培育激励机制和建立质量安全多元救济机制。

第六部分优化质量发展环境。从社会的角

度，提出了6个方面的举措，即：加强质量文化建设、营造良好市场环境、完善质量投诉和消费维权机制、发挥社会中介服务作用、加强质量舆论宣传和深化质量国际交流合作。

第七部分夯实质量发展基础。从质量基础建设的角度，提出了6个方面的工作，即：推进质量创新能力建设、加强标准化工作、强化计量基础支撑作用、推动完善认证认可体系、加快检验检测技术保障体系建设、推进质量信息化建设。

第八部分实施质量提升工程。从政府、行业、企业和社会多方面参与的角度，提出了5项重点工程，即：质量素质提升工程、可靠性提升工程、服务质量满意度提升工程、质量对比提升工程、清洁生产促进工程。

第九部分组织实施。从加强组织领导、完善配套政策、狠抓工作落实、强化检查考核等方面作了规定。特别提出要制定落实本《纲要》的年度行动计划，将落实质量发展的远期规划同解决当前突出的质量问题结合起来，使近期要求、实施步骤更有针对性，突出重点区域、重点领域、重点环节、重点产品和重点人群，有效解决事关公共安全、人身健康和生命财产安全的重点质量问题。

Circular of the State Council on Printing and Issuing the *Quality Development Outline* (*2011-2020*)

No. 9〔2012〕

To: The people's governments of all provinces, autonomous regions and municipalities directly under the Central Government, and ministries, commissions and bodies under the State Council,

The *Quality Development Outline* (*2011-2020*) is hereby printed and issued for earnest implementation.

The State Council
February 6, 2012

Quality Development Outline

(2011-2020)

This Outline is formulated for the purpose of thoroughly putting into practice the scientific thinking on development, promoting the transformation of the pattern of economic development, improving the overall quality level in our country and achieving sound and rapid economic and social development.

Ⅰ. Basis and Environment of Quality Development

Quality development is strategically crucial to the building of a prosperous and strong country. Quality reflects the overall strength of a country, the core competitiveness of enterprises and industries, as well as the civilization level of a nation. Quality is the integration of various elements including technology innovation, resource allocation and quality of workforce and is the comprehensive reflection of various aspects including legal environment, culture and education, trustworthiness and creditability building, etc. Quality is a strategic issue in economic and social development and is closely related to the sustainable development, the interests of the people, and the image of a country.

The Communist Party of China and the Chinese government have been attaching great importance to the quality development. Since the foundation of the People's Republic of China, especially since the reform and opening-up, an array of policies and measures has been worked out and implemented by the State, and a pattern of quality development with Chinese characteristics has taken shape. In particular, after the issuance and implementation of the "*Quality Invigoration Outline (1996-2010)*" by the State Council, the people's quality awareness has been raised constantly, the social environment for quality development optimized gradually, and the overall quality of the main industries and the quality management level of enterprises enhanced greatly. China has seen remarkable improvement in product quality, engineering project quality and service quality, and the quality of raw materials, basic components and parts, major equipment, consumer products and high-tech products has approached the average level of developed countries. The quality of a number of key national projects has reached the advanced level in the world. The quality of modern service industries, such as business and commerce, tourism, finance and logistics, has been improved notably. A standards system covering the primary, secondary and tertiary industries as well as the social undertakings has taken shape. Nevertheless, the basis for quality development is still weak in China, and the progress of quality improvement is still lagging behind the economic growth. The phenomena of stressing growth speed and quantity while neglecting quality and effectiveness still exist. The quality problems of products and engineering projects still cause fairly severe economic losses, environmental pollution and resource waste. Quality and safety accidents, especially food safety accidents, occur from time to time. Lacking credibility and trustworthiness, some manufacturers and business operators produce and sell forged and inferior products, which impair the market order and the social fairness, threaten the lives, health and safety of the people, and even harm the creditability and image of the country.

The second decade of the 21st century is a key stage to China for building a moderately prosperous society in all respects and accelerating socialist modernization. This period is also crucial for deepening reform and opening-up and speeding up the transformation of the pattern of economic development. At this important historical phase, the economic globalization is being further deepened, science and technology are advancing with each passing day, and the global industrial division and the structure of market demands are undergoing remarkable changes. Competition, with quality as the core element, is increasingly intense in aspects of standards, talents, technologies, market and resources. Meanwhile, given that China is expediting the process of industrialization, informatization, urbanization, marketization and its integration to the world, the solid quality basis becomes a necessity for achieving sound and rapid development, and quality work must fulfill higher requirements to meet the people's increasing demands for good quality. In the face of the new situation and new challenges, we must adhere to the strategy of "win with good quality" and build a strong country in respect of quality. This becomes an urgent necessity for ensuring and improving people's livelihood, an intrinsic requirement for adjusting the economic structure and transforming the pattern of development, a strategic choice of realizing scientific development and building a moderately prosperous society in all respects, and a prerequisite for improving the overall strength of the country and realizing the great rejuvenation of the Chinese nation.

Ⅱ. Guiding Principles, Working Guidelines and Development Objectives

(Ⅰ) **Guiding Principles.** Holding high the great banner of socialism with Chinese characteristics, following the guidance of the Deng Xiaoping's theory and the important thoughts of "Three Represents", and thoroughly putting into practice the scientific thinking on development, we should emphasize the rule of law, fulfill responsibilities properly, strengthen public education on quality, and raise quality awareness of the whole society. We should be far-sighted while grounded on current situations, push forward the overall while highlighting the key issues, and take comprehensive measures to treat both manifestation and root, so as to promote the building of a strong country in respect of quality and promote sound and rapid economic and social development.

(Ⅱ) **Working Guidelines.** People-oriented, safety-prioritizing, credibility and law-abiding, foundation-consolidating, innovation-driven, and winning with good quality.

——People-oriented should be taken as the value

orientation of quality development. The quality development shall meet the ever-growing material and cultural needs of the people, and better ensure and improve people's livelihood. It calls for concerted efforts of the people to improve the quality level and promote quality development.

——Safety-prioritizing should be taken as the basic requirement for quality development. In order to ensure in real earnest the health, lives and property safety of the people, the awareness of quality and safety should be enhanced; quality and safety responsibilities should be clearly prescribed and undertaken; supervision over quality and safety should be performed strictly; risk management of quality and safety should be reinforced; quality and safety assurance ability should be improved; and quality and safety incidents should be handled in a science-based manner.

——Creditability and law-abiding should be taken as the important foundation of quality development. Trustworthiness, credibility and lawful business operation should be advocated. The awareness of quality creditability should be enhanced; the quality creditability system should be optimized; illegal activities relating to quality should be cracked down stringently; the role of market system should be brought into full play; a market environment of fair competition should be created, which would foster the prosperity of the superior quality and elimination of the inferior; and an advanced quality culture should be cultivated.

——Foundation-consolidating should be taken as the assurance condition of quality development. Theoretical research and study should be conducted; the building of the rule of law on quality should be reinforced; quality management basis should be consolidated; more training of personnel engaged in quality work should be provided; capacity building in standardization, metrology, certification and accreditation, and inspection and testing should be promoted; and systems and mechanisms conducive to quality development should be continuously improved.

——Innovation-driven should be taken as a powerful driving force for quality development. Technological advancement should be accelerated; managerial innovation should be conducted; the quality of workforce should be improved; resource allocation should be optimized; innovative capability should be strengthened; and development vitality should be intensified. In doing so, we endeavor to develop the quality undertaking in a comprehensive, coordinated and sustainable manner.

——Winning with good quality should be taken as the core concept of quality development. While quality should be always kept as the priority, efficiency should be pursued in addition. The quality management level of all sectors should be improved in an all-round way; the strategic, fundamental and supporting roles of quality should be put into full play; the advantage in competitiveness should be built on high quality; and the core competitiveness of products, enterprises and industries of our country should be increased.

(Ⅲ) **Development Objectives.** By the year of 2020, notable achievements will be made in the building of a strong country in respect of quality, the quality foundation will be further consolidated, overall quality level will be markedly improved, and the achievements in quality development will benefit all the people. A number of advantageous enterprises with internationally renowned brands and core competitiveness will come into being; a group of modernized enterprises and industrial clusters with outstanding brand images, complete service platforms, and advanced quality level will emerge; and a testing system on food quality and safety and key products quality will be preliminarily set up. Thus a solid foundation of quality will take shape for the building of a moderately prosperous society in all respects and realizing the socialist modernization by the middle of the 21st century.

1. Product Quality: By the year of 2020, the product quality assurance system will be further optimized, the quality and safety indicators will meet the requirements set by the national compulsory standards in an all-round way; the quality innovation capability and competitiveness of Chinese original brands will be increased notably; varieties, quality and profits will be improved markedly; the performance in energy conservation and environmental protection will be enhanced drastically; and the people's increasing demands on quality will be basically met. Agricultural and food products will be high-quality, ecologically-sound and safe, and the product quality in the major manufacturing industries and the emerging strategic industries will reach or approach the advanced level in the world.

The detailed objectives of quality development by the year of 2015 are as follows:

——The quality and safety level of agricultural and food products will be steadily improved. The popularization rate of standardized agricultural production will exceed 30%. The pass rate of quality and safety random checking of main agricultural products will be stabilized at 96% or above. The quality and safety of key food products will be maintained in a good and stable state. Thus the quality and safety of agricultural and food products will be effectively guaranteed.

——The quality level of the manufacturing industries will be raised significantly. The conformity rate of product quality will be steadily increased, among which the pass rate of national supervision and random checking will be stably kept above 90%, the loss rate of major industrial products due to quality defection will be decreased gradually, the quality competitiveness will be improved, and the technical and quality indicators of key industrial products, such as key spare parts of major equipment, basic components and parts and basic materials, and important consumer products will reach or approach the advanced level in the world. A number of Chinese original brands with international competitiveness will be cultivated, and the brand value and profits will be increased notably.

——The development competence of the emerging strategic industries will be greatly improved. China will play a leading role in the development of a number of international standards; the quality of our main products will attain the advanced level in the world; a number of enterprises will be cultivated, among which the large-scaled ones will be characterized by high quality, influential brands and strong core competitiveness, and the small and medium-sized ones will be full of vigor in promoting innovation; and the emerging strategic industries will be promoted to becoming leading and pillar industries.

2. Engineering Project Quality: By the year of 2020, the quality of engineering projects will steadily improve, the quality of key national projects will reach the advanced level in the world, and people's satisfaction with project quality will increase greatly.

The detailed objectives of project quality development by the year of 2015 are as follows:

——The quality of engineering projects will improve markedly. The overall quality of engineering projects will undergo a steady improvement; durability and safety of important projects in building construction, transportation, water conservancy, electric power, etc. will be generally improved; the common quality defects will be rectified significantly; the pass rate of first-time acceptance examination of large and medium-sized engineering projects will reach 100%, and that of other projects will reach 98% or above. People's satisfaction with project quality (especially that of residential buildings) will increase notably, and complaints on construction projects will decrease year after year.

——Capability of technology innovation on engineering

project quality will be strengthened greatly. Core technologies will be developed and possessed in important engineering fields such as building construction, traffic infrastructure, clean energy and new energy; and the high technologies applied in energy conservation, environmental protection, security and information technology will increase notably. The energy efficiency and level of industrialized construction in construction projects will increase continuously. The eco-friendly construction will develop rapidly and performance of residential buildings will improve markedly.

3. Service Quality: By the year of 2020, standardization, normalization and branding will be applied in service quality in an overall way, and the quality level of the service industry will be improved greatly. A series of national pilot programs on comprehensive service standardization will be launched; the quality of mainstay service enterprises and key service projects will reach or approach the advanced level in the world; the brand value and profits of the service industry will increase drastically; and extensive development of the service industry will thus be facilitated.

The detailed objectives of quality development of the service industry by the year of 2015 are as follows:

——The quality of service catering to production will achieve an overall improvement. Standards systems will be set up and optimized in such key services catering to production as financial service, modern logistics, high-tech service, business service, transportation, and information service; and the national standards on service quality will be implemented generally in these fields. The emphasis will be placed on promoting the professional service quality in areas of out-sourcing, research and design, inspection and testing, after-sale service, credit rating, brand value evaluation, certification and accreditation, etc. Additional efforts will be made to integrate the service industry catering to production with the advanced manufacturing industry. A number of large service enterprises (groups) will be fostered, which will have great brand influence and strong competitiveness in quality. The customer satisfaction index in the service industry catering to production will reach 80 or above.

——The quality of service industry catering to people's living will achieve a notable improvement. The quality standards will keep pace with the advanced level in the world in such fields as wholesale, retail, accommodation, catering, residential service, tourism, family service, culture, sports, etc. The standards coverage will be expanded drastically, and national-grade demonstration zones on service standardization will be set up. A number of service brands and premium service projects with ethnic and cultural features will emerge; specialization, branding and networking will basically be applied as the operational modes; and the service varieties will be enriched to meet diversified demands of the people. Sectoral self-discipline and awareness of quality creditability will be strengthened markedly. The customer satisfaction index in the service industry catering to people's living will reach 75 or above.

Column 1-Main Indexes of Quality Development	
01	Product Quality(Year of 2015) The popularization rate of standardized agricultural production will exceed 30%. The pass rate in quality and safety random checking of major agricultural products will be steadily above 96%. The pass rate in the national supervision and random checking will be steadily above 90%.
02	Engineering Project Quality (Year of 2015) The pass rate of first-time acceptance examination of large and medium-sized engineering projects will reach 100%. The pass rate of first-time acceptance examination of other projects will reach 98% or above.
03	Service Quality(Year of 2015) The customer satisfaction rate of the service industry catering to production will reach 80 or above. The customer satisfaction rate of the service industry catering to people's living will reach 75 or above.

Ⅲ. Intensifying the Major Role of Enterprises in Quality

(Ⅰ) To be strict with enterprises as the main responsible party for quality. The responsibility system of critical control posts for quality and safety should be established. The legal representative or the principal responsible person shall assume the principal responsibility for quality and safety, and the quality managers shall assume the direct responsibility. The quality bylaws and the quality assessment system should be implemented strictly, and "power to veto" for quality and safety should be put in place. Enterprises should strictly carry out the rules on major quality accident reporting and the emergency management system, optimize the quality traceability system, and undertake in real earnest their quality guarantee responsibility, their statutory obligations such as defective product recall, and their legal liability in compensation for damages resulting from quality problems.

(Ⅱ) To improve the quality management of enterprises. Enterprises should establish and improve their quality management system; reinforce the all-dimensional quality management throughout all the processes and with involvement of all the employees; strictly organize the production and operation in line with the standards; perform strict quality control, quality check, measurement and testing; promote vigorously advanced technical measures and modern quality management concepts and methods; and conduct extensive activities of quality improvement, quality breakthroughs, quality comparison, quality risk analysis, quality cost control, quality management work in teams, etc. We should also apply actively environment-friendly technologies such as quantity reduction, waste reclamation, re-cycling, re-utilization, re-manufacturing, etc., and develop vigorously low-carbon, cleaner and high-efficiency operational modes.

(Ⅲ) To accelerate innovation by enterprises in quality technologies. Technological innovation should be considered as a necessary tool for quality improvement. More input should be given to technological innovation, and application of scientific and technical achievements should be accelerated. Standardization and patent registration of innovative achievements should be emphasized. Such situations should be changed as " attending to manufacturing whereas neglecting research and development "," attending to technology introduction whereas neglecting practical application ", and "attending to imitation whereas neglecting innovation". New technologies, new processing techniques and new materials should be actively put in to use; quality and varieties of products should be improved; product grades and service levels should be raised; innovative products and services with core competitiveness, high added value, and independent intellectual property rights should be researched and developed. Competent enterprises should be encouraged to set up their own technical centers, engineering centers and industrialization bases and be fostered into innovative enterprises combining research, development, design, manufacturing and system integration.

(Ⅳ) **To bring the leading role of advantageous enterprises into full play.** Efforts should be made to promote central enterprises and mainstay enterprises in various sectors to become major participants in the development of international standards and the main entities to implement national and sectoral standards. The successful experience and advanced methods of quality management should be popularized and extended to both ends of the industry chain, in order to promote an upgrading of the overall quality. The role of advantageous enterprises should be brought into full play in guiding and driving the small and medium-sized ones; formulation of the standards for enterprises alliance should be encouraged; new product development and brand building should be guided; the small and medium-sized enterprises should be urged to implement technical upgrading and managerial innovation; and the level of professional division and coordination and the market service ability should be improved, so as to improve their competitiveness in respect of quality.

(Ⅴ) **To promote enterprises to fulfill their social responsibilities.** The concept of ensuring quality and safety and promoting sustainable development should be intensified as the social responsibilities of enterprises; the mechanism for fulfilling social responsibilities should be established and improved; and the fulfillment of social responsibilities should be incorporated into the operational and managerial decision-making of enterprises. Enterprises should be urged to actively fulfill their social responsibilities to the stake-holders such as employees, consumers, investors, partners, community and environment. Enterprises should also be encouraged to publish their social responsibility reports, strengthen their creditability and self-discipline, honor their quality commitments, create a comprehensive value in the economic, environmental and social aspects, and set up a responsible image to society.

Ⅳ. Strengthening Quality Supervision and Administration

(Ⅰ) **To accelerate the building of the rule of law in terms of quality.** The concept of the rule of law in terms of quality should be firmly built, and the prominent contradictions and problems in quality development should be resolved through legal means. Laws and regulations on quality and safety and quality liability investigation should be studied, drawn up and improved, whereby legal framework on quality is bettered. Law-based administration should be conducted strictly and law enforcement should follow a well-defined code of conduct to ensure that the law is enforced in a strict, fair and civilized manner. Building of law enforcement teams should be strengthened through education and training of law enforcement personnel and the improvement of their comprehensive quality and law enforcement ability. The supervisory mechanism on the quality legal system should be improved and the law enforcement responsibilities should be fulfilled, whereby liability goes with powers, use of powers is supervised, compensation is paid for tort and offenders are prosecuted. Publicity and education in the legal system of quality should be intensified, the legal knowledge on quality should be popularized, and a good social environment for learning, using and abiding by the law should be created.

(Ⅱ) **To strengthen quality and safety supervision.** The national catalogue of key products under supervision should be formulated and implemented, and the supervision and control should be strengthened on key products, major equipment, important engineering projects and significant service items vital to the people's livelihood, health and safety, energy conservation and environmental protection. Supervisory checks should be intensified on food, pharmaceuticals, articles for women, children and the elderly, agricultural means of production, building materials, important consumer goods and emergency supplies. Supervisory systems should be improved in fields of production licensing, compulsory product certification, supervision and administration of major equipment, statutory inspection of import and export commodities, safety supervision and registration of special equipment, etc. Special attention should be paid to key areas such as rural markets and markets in fringe zones between city and countryside. The quality and safety supervision in production, circulation and import & export should be enhanced, the traceability of product quality and safety should be enhanced, a liaison system of quality and safety should be established, and the long-term mechanism for quality and safety supervision should be improved.

(Ⅲ) **To implement quality and safety risk management.** The major quality accident reporting system and the product injury monitoring system should be established by enterprises. Risk monitoring and risk analysis and assessment should be strengthened for key products, key sectors and key areas. Timely early-warnings should be given upon occurrence of regional, sectoral and systematic quality risks. The measures for handling major potential risks in quality and safety should be proposed in a timely manner. Such systems should be established and improved as the preventive system against alien harmful animals and plants, the quality and safety assurance system for import and export agricultural and food products, the quality and safety monitoring system for import and export industrial products and the risk monitoring system of frontier health quarantine, so as to effectively reduce the entry-exit risks of animal and plant epidemics, ensure the quality and safety of import and export agricultural, food and industrial products, and prevent cross-border spread of infectious diseases. Actions should be taken to improve the mechanism of quality and safety risk management, develop the contingency plan for quality and safety risks, strengthen the sharing of risk information and resources, improve the capability of risk prevention and emergency response, and practice the early identification, early judgments, early warning, and early handling of quality and safety risks in earnest.

Column 2-Establishment and Improvement of Quality and Safety Risk Management System	
01	To Strengthen the Early-warning system for Food Quality and Safety Risks Organize the implementation of concentrated, efficient and targeted food safety risk early-warning and improve functions of information collection, risk monitoring, and early-warning notification on food safety. Emphasize the building of the food safety risk monitoring network, strengthen the monitoring of illegal additives and food additives, carry out safety assessment in a timely manner and effectively guard against the systematic risks.

Column 2-Establishment and Improvement of Quality and Safety Risk Management System	
02	To Improve the Product Injury Monitoring System The competent departments such as quality supervision and inspection and quarantine, health, etc. should join their efforts to establish a product injury monitoring system, collect and carry out statistics and analysis of injury information related to products, evaluate the potential risks of product safety, issue product injury early-warnings in a timely manner, and provide basis for governmental departments, industry organizations and enterprises to develop precautionary measures.
03	To Strengthen the Risk Early-warning System for Product Quality and Safety Build the information collection network for product quality and safety, establish a system for monitoring public opinions on product quality and safety, improve public technical services of risk early-warning, strengthen risk monitoring of high-risk industries, key products and import and export commodities, and improve effectiveness of risk assessment and early-warning for product quality and safety.
04	To Improve the Epidemic Risk Monitoring of Entry and Exit Animal and Plant Quarantine and Frontier Health Quarantine Improve the information collection network of epidemic risks in entry and exit animal and plant quarantine and frontier health quarantine; fulfill the function of providing public technology and information service concerning standards and regulations on entry and exit animal and plant quarantine, risk monitoring, risk assessment, risk early-warning, epidemic information, and quarantine interception; and enhance capability of health quarantine and animal and plant quarantine at ports.

(Ⅳ) **To strengthen macro-quality statistical analysis.** We shall establish and improve the quality index system the main contents of which include the quality conformity rate of products, the quality conformity rate of export commodities, the customer satisfaction index and the loss rate due to defection. Efforts should be made to promote incorporation of the quality indexes into the statistical index system of national economic and social development. Every region and every sector should, in line with its actual situation, establish and improve the analysis and reporting system on quality status, conduct periodical assessment and analysis on quality status and quality competitiveness, undertake comparative studies of quality development trends at home and abroad, and provide basis for macroeconomic decision-making.

(Ⅴ) **To promote the building of the quality creditability system.** The system for collection and release of quality credit information should be improved. The quality credit information platform should be established, taking the real-name registration of organization codes as the foundation and the article numbering management as the traceability means. Quality credit building in each sector should be promoted, and quality credit information should be exchanged and shared among various departments such as banks, commerce, customs, taxation, industry and commerce, quality supervision and inspection and quarantine, industry, agriculture, insurance, and statistics. The enterprise dossier of quality credit and the records of product quality credit information should be improved, the quality credit evaluation system should be enhanced, and the classified supervision over quality credit should be enforced. Those breaking the quality credit should be blacklisted and publicized, and tougher penalties should be imposed on them. Growth of service institutions on quality credit should be encouraged and development of quality credit evaluation institutions should be well defined; popularized use of products with good quality credit should be promoted; and a multi-level, all-dimensional quality credit service market should be established.

(Ⅵ) **To severely crack down on quality violations in accordance with law.** Governance at the production origin should be strengthened, market supervision and administration should be intensified, quality law enforcement on key products and key projects and in key industries, key areas and key markets should be carried out in depth, serious and major cases of manufacturing and selling counterfeits should be rigorously investigated and dealt with, unlawful acts endangering public security, people's health, life and property safety should be severely cracked down, and illegal activities on quality by means of high technology should be stringently investigated and prosecuted. Law enforcement cooperation should be strengthened; the quick response mechanism and the law enforcement cooperation mechanism for handling severe emergency cases of quality violation should be established and improved; the centralized rectification of product quality problems with common sectoral or regional characteristics should be strengthened; and campaigns should be organized in depth against counterfeited products such as agricultural means of production and building materials, so as to protect the legitimate rights and interests of the people. A reward system to quality and safety reports should be established and improved, and the commitment to the informant of rewarding should be earnestly fulfilled, and the legitimate rights and interests of the informant should be protected. Transfer and connection between administrative law enforcement and criminal justice should be conducted effectively, and the efforts in criminal justice to crack down on quality violations should be intensified.

Ⅴ. Making Innovation in the Mechanism of Quality Development

(Ⅰ) **To improve the system and mechanisms of the quality work.** The quality macro-management system with Chinese characteristics and in line with requirements of socialist market economic development should be improved. The quality and safety responsibility system should be improved, in which the local government takes the overall responsibility, the competent departments take their respective responsibilities, and enterprises take the primary responsibility. A quality work pattern should be built, in which the government exercises supervision, the market plays the role of regulation, enterprises function as primary players, the sectors performs self-discipline and society participates therein. We should make full use of economic, legal and administrative means to maintain quality and safety. The active role of market and enterprises in promoting quality development should be brought into full play. The governmental input should be increased in the comprehensive quality administration and the quality and safety assurance capability; the administrative resources should be rationally allocated; the quality infrastructure construction should be strengthened; duty performance of the quality supervision departments should be enhanced; and institutions of quality supervision and technical service should be gradually established in functional zones, such as economic and technical development zones and high-tech industrial parks, and townships clustered with industries. The activities of building a strong province (region, city) in respect of quality should be extensively carried out, and thus concerted administration and control over quality by the whole society would be formed.

(Ⅱ) **To improve the quality evaluation and appraisal mechanism.** A scientific and standardized quality performance evaluation and appraisal system should be established and improved; the quality evaluation indicators and the appraisal system of people's governments at all levels and the relevant sectors should be bettered; and the quality safety and quality development should be incorporated into the performance appraisal of the people's governments at all levels. The feedback of the appraisal results should be enhanced; the application of the results should be strengthened; and the performance appraisal results should constitute an index for the comprehensive assessment of the leadership team and the leading cadres, which should be used as a reference for leadership team building and selection, appointment, training and education, management and supervision, incentives for and constraints on leading cadres. Quality accidents should be investigated seriously and accountability should be investigated strictly. Warning accountability and supervisory rectification should be strengthened. Malpractice and corruption involved in quality accidents should be severely investigated and dealt with.

(Ⅲ) **To strengthen the quality access and withdrawal mechanism.** The function of quality supervision should be exercised. With regard to sectors and products with heavy pollution, high energy consumption, heavy emission and resource waste, market access should be strictly regulated, elimination of outdated production capacity should be speeded up, and the structural optimization and upgrading should be promoted. Stricter quality access conditions and higher market access threshold should be laid down for products vital to human health and property safety and the important and sensitive import and export commodities. The recall system for products with defects and unsafe food products should be established and improved. Enterprises which fail to meet the access conditions, fail to ensure quality and safety or fail to meet the requirements even after rectification should withdraw from the market according to law. Those committing severe violations should be banned.

(Ⅳ) **To make innovation on the incentive mechanism for quality development.** The national and regional quality award systems should be established, so as to commend and award the organizations and individuals with advanced quality management and remarkable achievements, to set advanced examples, and to encourage enterprises and the whole society to attend to quality, stress on trustworthiness and creditability and foster strong brand names. National funds for SME development should provide aid to small and medium-sized enterprises for product research and development and quality breakthroughs. Enterprises should be encouraged to actively compete for the honor of the advanced work-team on quality management and the quality pacesetter, and the quality personnel should be encouraged to strive for the "May 1st" Labor Medal.

(Ⅴ) **To create an incentive mechanism for brand cultivation.** The brand development strategy should be vigorously implemented, the leading role of brand should be brought into full play; rules and measures for brand cultivation and development should be developed and enforced; and the building of famous brands should be carried out. More efforts should be made to protect independent intellectual property rights, and the long-lasting mechanism and favorable environment for brand development should be fostered. Supports should be provided to enterprises for opening up overseas markets by relying on technical standards, implementing the branding operation and the marketing diversification strategy, and fostering internationally well-known brands. The national standards system of brand building and the brand value evaluation system should be established. The brand value evaluation system should be improved to be in conformity with the international standards, and the right to have a say in international brand value evaluation should be strengthened. Work should be further intensified in the development of products of geographical indication, time-honored trademarks in China and regionally famous brand-name products.

Column 3-Key Measures for Brand Building	
01	To Establish the Standards System in Brand Building Take quality as the core to strengthen brand cultivation, brand management and brand evaluation methodology study, develop national standards in brand terminology, key elements, evaluation requirements, and building guidelines, etc. , and establish the national standards system in brand building commensurate with China's circumstances and consistent with the international standards.
02	To Establish the Brand Value Evaluation System Take the consumer acceptance and the survival in market competition as the fundamental principles and, with reference to international standards and international common practices, take the monetary value evaluation of brand as the main contents and highlight such competitive industries as equipment manufacturing, non-ferrous iron and steel, textile and garment, light industry and household appliances, electronic information, automobile manufacturing, petro-chemistry, modern logistics and tourism, so as to establish a brand value evaluation system with Chinese characteristics and improve the internationalization level of Chinese brands.

Column 3-Key Measures for Brand Building	
03	To Build Famous Brands Formulate the conditions for brand building and the supporting policies and measures and focus on industry cluster areas, national innovation demonstration zones, economic and technological development zones, high-tech industrial parks, modern service areas and tourist destinations to prompt local people's governments to build famous brands, regulate the sectoral development, expand brand influence and enhance the competitiveness of regional economy.

(Ⅵ) **To develop diversified remedies for quality and safety.** Active efforts should be made to put into practice diversified remedies for product quality and safety that are in conformity with the market economy rules and conducive to consumer rights protection. The infringement accountability system should be improved, and the insurance system of product quality and safety liability should be set up to ensure that the victims of quality and safety accidents get reasonable and timely compensation. Enterprises, industry associations, insurance and evaluation institutions should be guided to strengthen cooperation, reduce quality and safety risks, and earnestly safeguard the legitimate rights and interests of enterprises and consumers.

Ⅵ. To Optimize the Environment for Quality Development

(Ⅰ) **To strengthen the building of quality culture.** The

concept that quality is the lifeline of an enterprise should be firmly rooted and the business strategy of " win with good quality" should be implemented. The quality spirit of trustworthiness and creditability, continuous improvement, innovation and development, and pursuit of excellence should be transformed into the code of conduct of society, enterprises and their employees, who consequently will resist illegal activities of production and business operation in good consciousness. Steps should be taken to promote the building of an advanced socialist quality culture, to increase quality awareness of the people, to advocate the concepts of being scientific and rational, quality and safe, energy saving and environment friendly, to strive for creating the favorable atmosphere in which the government prioritize quality, enterprises pursue quality, society advocates quality, and every person cares about quality, and to improve the soft power of quality culture.

(Ⅱ) **To create a favorable market environment.** Such an environment should be created in which various types of enterprises would use the means of production lawfully, participate in market competition fairly, and be protected by law equally. Quality and safety should be considered as an active element of expanding market demands, and efforts should be made to further release the consumption potentials of urban and rural residents, and to promote the flow and clustering of social resources towards quality products, outstanding brands and competitive enterprises. Actions should be taken to combat monopoly and unfair competition, eradicate resolutely the local protection, safeguard the market order, and create a fair and orderly market environment prospering the superior quality and eliminating the inferior. Enterprises should be guided to participate in international cooperation and exchanges, build good international images for Chinese enterprises and products, and enhance the international competitiveness.

(Ⅲ) **To improve the mechanism of quality complaints and consumer right protection.** Quality complaint handling institutions should be enhanced, which would use modern information technology to improve the quality complaint information platform, bring into full play the role of complaint hotlines such as 12365, 12315, etc., and ensure unblocked channels for quality complaints and consumer right protection. Quality-concerned arbitrational inspection and identification should be promoted actively in order to effectively mediate and handle quality disputes and resolve social conflicts. The public awareness of quality right protection should be enhanced and a social quality-supervisor system be established. Consumers should be supported and encouraged to protect their quality rights according to law, so as to better safeguard the rights and interests of users and consumers.

(Ⅳ) **To bring the role of social intermediary services into full play.** Organizational building of social intermediary services should be strengthened in the fields of quality management, inspection and testing, measurement and calibration, conformity assessment and credit rating in order to promote the development of the quality service market. Monitoring of and guidance to the quality service market should be enhanced, integration and restructuring should be encouraged, large-scale operation, networking and brand building of quality service bodies should be promoted, and Chinese original brands of quality service should be cultivated. Industry associations, societies, chambers of commerce and other social groups should actively provide consultation services on technologies, standards, quality management and brand building, duly reflect the quality demands of enterprises and consumers, establish the self-discipline operational mechanism according to the market rules, further promote the normalized development of the service industry, and bring into full play the bridging and linking role of intermediary organizations in quality development.

(Ⅴ) **To strengthen publicity on quality.** Intensive efforts should be made to carry out quality activities for the public with abundant contents and in diverse forms such as the national "Quality Month", the "March · 15th" International Consumer Rights Protection Day, etc., and disseminate the fundamental quality knowledge in enterprises, institutions, communities and countryside. Correct guidance of public opinions should be insisted on; working policies and guidelines, laws and regulations on quality and models of quality management should be vigorously publicized; quality surveillance by public opinions should be strengthened; and efforts in exposure of quality violation cases should be increased to combat quality violations. The role of news media as the leading channel in publicity should be brought into full play, and various kinds of media should be guided to report quality problems in an objective manner.

(Ⅵ)**To promote international exchanges and cooperation on quality.** Steps should be taken to actively attend and host international quality conferences, exchange the achievements in quality management and technologies, and develop pragmatic cooperation. On the basis of the key industrial and regional economic development outlines and the consistency in inspection and testing technologies and standards, such activities should be conducted as establishing bilateral and multi-lateral cooperative and consultative mechanisms in quality, participating in the development of quality-related international and regional standards, rules and regulations, and facilitating the integration of Chinese systems of standards, metrology, certification and accreditation into the international regime. We should make active responses to the technical trade measures adopted by foreign countries and improve the technical trade measures of our own. Domestic enterprises, research institutes, academies, colleges, universities, and public entities should be encouraged to carry out international exchanges and cooperation on quality and introduce advanced foreign quality management methodology, technologies and high-caliber talents.

Ⅶ. Consolidating the Foundation of Quality Development

(Ⅰ)**To promote the building of quality innovation capacity.** We should increase the input in quality technologies, intensify the building of quality research institutions, launch academic programs for quality education, form a multi-level pattern for training of quality personnel, foster a group of leading talents in quality technologies, explore and establish the quality management theory, methodology and technology system with Chinese characteristics, and intensify conversion and application of quality technological achievements. We should speed up the building of a system of quality technology innovation, under which enterprises function as the main party, the market provides orientation, and the production are combined with learning and research. Those advanced enterprises, key research institutions, colleges and universities should use their advantaged position in accumulation of innovative elements to build quality innovation bases that are characterized by clear emphases, complementary advantages and resource-sharing. Implementation of significant programs of quality improvement and technical reform should be promoted, and new advantages in respect of quality should be cultivated with technologies, standards, branding and service as the core.

(Ⅱ) **To strengthen the standardization work.** Construction of the national standards system should be accelerated in the fields of modern agriculture, advanced manufacturing, emerging strategic industries, modern service industry, energy conservation and emissions reduction, social administration, public service, and so on. The standards classification management should be implemented, and the management of compulsory standards should be reinforced. The standards shall be formulated and revised at shorter intervals, and the vanguard nature, effectiveness and applicability of standards should be improved. We should adopt international standards in a proactive manner, enhance our ability to substantially participate in international standardization activities, promote the conversion of Chinese advantageous technologies and standards into international standards, participate actively in the development and revision of the international standards which impact the related industry development in China, and improve the ability to cope with global competition in technical standards. Efforts should be made to improve the standardization management system, promote innovation on the standardization working mechanism, strengthen the effective connection between standardization and policies on technological, economic and social development, and facilitate the effective combination of the military and the civil standardization work. A supporting system and a public service system of standardization technologies should be built and the service platform of national technical standards resources should be bettered.

Column 4-Key Points of the Standardization Work	
01	Modern Agriculture Improve the agricultural standards system covering the conditions of agricultural materials, agricultural infrastructure, production technologies, product quality, transportation and storage, market trade, agricultural product quality inspection, prevention and control of animal and plant epidemics, and agricultural social service; and study and formulate technical standards supporting high-yield, good-quality, efficient, eco-friendly, and safe agricultural production.

Column 4-Key Points of the Standardization Work	
02	Emerging Strategic Industries Formulate the standardization construction outline for emerging strategic industries, accelerate the building of a standards system conducive to development of these industries, and launch pilot programs for formulating the standards thereon.
03	Modern Service Industry Actively enlarge the standardization scope in the service industry; establish and improve the quality standards and sectoral norms which refine and deepen the division of productive service; draw up and improve the standards on services catering to people's living; establish and improve the national standards system of service quality featuring clear focus, reasonable structure, and scientific applicability; realize a 100% coverage of standards in important service sectors and key service fields; and expand the coverage of service standards.
04	Energy Conservation and Emissions Reduction Establish and improve the standards system in resources, energy and environment; focus on research and development of such standards conducive to resource conservation as the advanced technical standards, the energy efficiency standards for leading runners, the energy consumption quotas for high-energy consumption products, the energy efficiency standards for end energy-using products, fuel consumption thresholds for vehicles, water consumption quotas, and recycling and reuse standards for waste; and optimize the standards system for resource conservation.

Column 4-Key Points of the Standardization Work	
05	Social Management Establish and improve the standardization system covering education, health, population, public employment and talent service, labor relations, social insurance, social management, etc. , so as to promote social fairness and justice and the building of a harmonious society.
06	Demonstration and Pilot Standardization Programs Foster a number of national-level standardization demonstration zones and pilot programs in fields of agriculture, service, circular economy, high technologies, national key projects, etc.

(Ⅲ) **To intensify the fundamental supporting role of metrology.** Keeping pace with the progress of new-type industrialization, we shall establish and improve the primary standards for measurement and the systems for dissemination of values of quantity and measurement traceability, which are based on the basis of quantum physics and characterized by high precision, high stability, and international consistency. Actions should be taken to closely follow the international development of cutting-edge metrological technologies, to meet emerging demands of measurement for national strategic new-industry development, energy conservation and emissions reduction, circular economy, fair trade, livelihood improvement, etc. , to intensify the building of the measuring standards, to push forward vigorously the legal metrology, strengthen comprehensively the industrial metrology, and expand actively the engineering metrology, to reinforce surveillance over energy metrology, to foster and normalize the calibration market, and to enhance the research and application of measurement testing technologies. Efforts should be made to promote the metrological service ability, establish a number of important basic facilities for precision measurement, and establish and better the national innovation bases of metrological technology and the service-sharing platforms. A metrology system adapting to the economic and social development should be set up without delay.

(Ⅳ) **To promote improvement of the certification and accreditation system.** We should, with reference to internationally accepted rules, establish and improve a managerial pattern of certification and accreditation, which integrates the rule of law, governance of administrative authorities, constraint of accreditation, self-discipline of the sectors, and supervision of society. Steps should be taken to improve the certification and accreditation system, strengthen the service capacity thereof, increase the effectiveness of compulsory product certification, promote a healthy and orderly development of voluntary product certification, and better the managerial system and the service certification system. Further efforts should be made to foster orderly certification and testing markets, and the supervision and administration on certifying bodies, laboratories, and inspection organizations shall be enforced. International mutual recognition should be steadily pushed forward, the rights to participate in and have a say on international rulemaking in certification and accreditation should be enhanced, and the international influence of China in the field will be increased.

Column 5-Key Points in the Work of Certification and Accreditation	
01	To Improve the Accreditation Capacity Research and develop new types of accreditation system, and promote the accreditation work in good agricultural practice (GAP), hazard analysis and critical control point (HACCP), energy conservation and emissions reduction in the field of food safety. Maintain a steady growth of laboratory accreditation in quantity and capacity.
02	To Optimize the Compulsory Product Certification Conduct analysis on quality status, risk assessment of safety, and public quality and safety evaluation on products under compulsory certification; enhance supervision and examination on certifying bodies and their staff, and certified enterprises and their products; improve the quality traceability system on products under compulsory certification, and thus promote the overall improvement in quality of certified products.
03	To Promote the Voluntary Product Certification Improve the national voluntary certification system; strengthen product certification in energy conservation, water conservation, electricity conservation, fuel conservation, renewable resources and environmental labeling; promote product certification of environment-friendly facilities and equipment for comprehensive utilization; enhance supervision over effectiveness of certification on organic products, green food, pollution-free farm products, etc.

Column 5-Key Points in the Work of Certification and Accreditation	
04	To Improve the Level of Management System Certification Deepen the management system certification on quality, environment, and occupational health and safety, strive to improve effectiveness of certification, actively expand certification fields, and promote broader application of management system standards in social management, culture, education, medical care and newly emerged industries; enhance research and development on the information technology services and on the system certification of supply-chain security.
05	To Improve the Information Security Certification and Accreditation System Intensify the system and competence building on information security certification and accreditation, improve the working system thereof, and promote social admissibility of the results thereof.
06	To Accelerate Implementation of Service Certification Speed up research, development and implementation of new service certification systems, and promote the establishment and implementation of certification and accreditation systems in such key fields as transportation, financial service, information service, commercial service, tourism, sports industry, etc.

(Ⅴ) **To speed up the building of a technological supporting system for inspection and testing.** We should promote resource integration among technical institutions, optimize the allocation of inspection and testing resources, build the platforms for sharing testing resources, improve the instant inspection and testing approaches for food and agricultural product quality, and enhance the inspection and testing ability. More efforts should be made to construct governmental laboratories and testing institutions, which will provide effective supervision over quality and safety of products vital to the national economy and the people's livelihood. A scientific, impartial and authoritative third-party inspection and testing system should be established, while technical institutions with various forms of ownership should be encouraged to equally engage in the market competition. Steps should be taken to provide classified guidance and supervision over different technical institutions, to standardize inspection and testing activities, to urge technical institutions to improve their internal management and incentive mechanism, raise the quality and service level of inspection and testing, and increase their creditability. Support should be given to technical institutions in implementing the strategy of "going out" and in the building of first-class international technical institutions.

Column 6-Improvement of Inspection and Testing Competence	
01	Research and Development of Testing Instruments and Facilities Reinforce the research and development of inspection and testing technologies and of testing facilities, promote domestic production of key testing facilities, and speed up the screening, popularization and application of instant testing instruments and facilities and testing methods.

Column 6-Improvement of Inspection and Testing Competence	
02	Building of Testing Institutions Promote the international mutual-recognition of laboratories, and build a number of high-level national product quality supervision and testing centers, key laboratories, and type evaluation laboratories, whereby central laboratories at local and regional levels cover various professions and have a reasonable geographical distribution.
03	Building of Platforms for Sharing Testing Resources Make more efforts to build public testing technology service platforms in industry cluster areas, and improve the ability to facilitate the testing service for small and medium-sized enterprises.
04	Building of Inspection and Quarantine Competence Improve the capability of responding to and implementing the technical trade measures, strengthen the monitoring on the entry-exit epidemics and improve the capacity building of import-export commodity inspection and testing technologies. Build a number of public testing technology service platforms catering for the entire chain from design and development, manufacturing to after-sale service at economic and technological development zones, hi-tech industrial parks and export processing zones. Set up a number of professional laboratory testing unions with independent brands.
05	Key Programs Carry out special capacity building programs for enhancing the overall competence of testing and risk monitoring on food quality and safety, and implement special programs on building quality testing systems for products and engineering projects in key industries.

(Ⅵ) **To promote the use of information technology in the work of quality.** Steps should be taken to expedite the building of a quality information network. By use of the internet of things and other information technology and with the support of the national fundamental-information resources such as article numbering and organization codes, the collection, tracing, analyses and processing on product and project quality information shall be strengthened, the use of information technology in quality control and management shall be enhanced, and the efficiency of dynamic monitoring on quality and safety, safety risk early-warning, emergency response, and quality credit management shall be raised. In-depth integration of information technology with industrialization should be promoted so as to enhance the use of information technology for promoting product and project quality.

Ⅷ. Carrying out Quality Enhancement Programs

(Ⅰ) **Quality attainment enhancement programs.** Measures including public and vocational education on quality knowledge and the training of specialized personnel should be taken to enhance the quality attainment of the entire population. Social practice bases of quality education should be established for primary and middle school students for the purpose of disseminating quality knowledge. Qualified higher-learning institutions should be encouraged to set up majors concerning quality-management and train personnel specialized in quality. A variety of training institutes for quality education should be established with a well-defined code of conduct to carry out enterprise-oriented quality trainings extensively, focus on strengthening quality management training of enterprise operators, strengthen the training in process specifications and operating technologies for front-line workers, and improve the quality awareness and quality skills of all staff in enterprises. By the year of 2015, fairly full-fledged systems at the national level should take form on occupational qualification for quality supervision personnel, plant engineering consultant registration and metrology engineer certification.

(Ⅱ) **Reliability enhancement programs.** Reliability enhancement programs should be implemented in key industries such as automobiles, machine tools, aeronautics and astronautics, ship building, track transportation, power-generating equipment, construction machinery, special equipment, household appliances, components and parts, and basic parts. Such work should be undertaken as strengthening the reliability design and experiment and the quality control during production, enhancing the reliability level through technological advancement, managerial innovation and standards improvement, and promoting the transformation of Chinese product quality from being conformity-oriented to applicability and reliability-oriented. By the year of 2020, the reliability level of Chinese basic parts, general-purpose parts and key parts of automatic measurement and control should meet the demands of the domestic market, and that of key products should reach or approach the advanced level in the world. The reliability of a batch of major equipment should reach the advanced level in the world such as 1000MW nuclear power equipment, new energy power generation equipment, high-speed EMU, high-grade CNC machine tools and basic manufacturing equipment.

(Ⅲ) **Customer satisfaction enhancement programs in service quality.** Systems of service standards and of service quality assessment should be formed and perfected on the basis of different characteristics of service industries catering to production and people's living. Systems of customer satisfaction assessment should be set up and pilot programs thereof should be launched in key fields such as transportation, modern logistics, banking and insurance, commerce and trade, tourism and accommodation, medical and health care, postal service and communications, community services, etc. Guidance should be offered to enterprises to improve their service quality, satisfy market demands, and thus promote the standardized, normalized and internationalized development of the service market.

(Ⅳ) **Programs of quality enhancement by comparison.** Activities of quality enhancement by comparison should be conducted extensively in different categories and at various levels in sectors of agriculture, industry, construction industry, service, etc. Performance comparisons of competitive nature should be carried out in key sectors and pillar industries with reference to the advanced level in the world and in China; and comparison in the process quality and in the managerial performance should be developed in key enterprises and products along the industrial chain and within the given regions. Such work should be done as establishing the working mechanisms of quality enhancement by comparison, formulating scientific assessment measures, and completing the quality comparison and analysis database, so as to provide reference and basis of quality improvement for framing development strategies and specifying development goals. Actions also should include establishing quality improvement and surpassing measures, improving production techniques, upgrading production facilities, making innovations on managerial patterns, and improving marketing strategies. Quality enhancement service platforms should be established, and the public service and social service systems providing information consultancy and technological support to small and medium-sized enterprises should be perfected, so as to realize the quality enhancement and surpassing. By the year of 2015, activities of quality enhancement by comparison would be carried out among 50,000 enterprises in important and key sectors, where by advanced quality management ideas spread extensively, scientific quality management methods and technologies are adopted generally, and the quality of the leading enterprises in mainstay and pillar industries reach the advanced level in the world.

(Ⅴ) **Programs for promotion of clean production.** The clean production should be promoted actively. Development and revision of standards related to energy conservation, emissions reduction and circular economy should be expedited, and the systems should be established and improved for low-carbon product labeling, energy efficiency labeling, recycled product labeling, low-carbon certification and energy-saving product certification. The financial and taxation policies preferential to clean production should be implemented and improved. Service platforms of clean production technologies should be set up, research and development of technologies of energy conservation and emissions reduction should be speeded up, and a number of key technical difficulties should be resolved. The surveillance system on energy metering should be formed, and the supervisory management on energy metering should be performed on key high-energy-consuming enterprises. The market access and withdrawal mechanism should be established, production licensing management should be tightened up towards high-energy-consuming and high-polluting projects, and outdated production capacity should be eliminated. By the year of 2015, the industrialization and standardization level of new technologies in clean production should be improved drastically, a number of demonstration projects and public service platforms in clean production should come into being, the formation and discharge of pollutants generated in the course of production should be brought under effective control, and the consumption of resources should fall greatly.

Ⅸ. Organization and Implementation

(Ⅰ) **To strengthen organization and leadership.** The competent department of the State Council in charge of quality should organize and host joint conferences in light of the work needs, strengthen the overall planning, organization and leadership of the quality work, formulate the annual action plans for implementation of this Outline, conduct research in, and coordinate efforts for, the handling of major quality issues, and urge and inspect the implementation of this Outline. The local people's governments at all levels and the departments in charge of different sectors should incorporate the quality development objectives into the national economic and social development planning of the respective regions or sectors in line with the arrangement and requirements of this Outline, strengthen the quality policy guidance, place the quality work at an important position on their working agenda, work out the implementation plans, specify goals and responsibilities, organize in earnest the corresponding implementation, and improve substantially the ability to organize and support quality development.

(Ⅱ) **To improve supporting policies.** In order to build a strong country in respect of quality, the local people's governments at all levels and the departments in charge of different sectors should work out, within their administrative areas or sectors, the supporting policies and measures for promotion of quality development, increase the input in the quality work, and improve the policies and measures concerning industries, environment, science and technology, finance, taxation, talent cultivation, etc. In the course of implementation, efforts should be made to increase the compatibility of the policies of this Outline with those specified in the Twelfth Five-Year Plan for National Economic and Social Development and other related plans, so as to ensure the fulfillment of all the goals and objectives provided in this Outline.

(Ⅲ) **To stress on implementation through practical work.** The local people's governments at all levels and the departments in charge of different sectors should combine the implementation of the long-term planning for quality development with the resolution of current prominent problems, so as to device in more pertinence the short-term requirements and the implementation steps, highlight the key regions, key sectors, key links, key products and key population groups, and effectively solve the major quality issues vital to public security, human health, life and property safety. All the local governments and all the departments concerned should implement the development goals and objectives and the main tasks set in this Outline and the annual action plans, taking into sufficient consideration their practical problems in quality and safety, so as to lay a solid quality foundation, ensure quality and safety and promote quality development.

(Ⅳ) **To strengthen checking and evaluation.** The local people's government at all levels and the departments in charge of different sectors should establish a responsibility system for implementing this Outline, conduct strict checking and evaluation on implementation of this Outline, strive to put earnestly all the work into effect, and ensure that quality development would yield substantial outcomes. Units and individuals making outstanding achievements in the implementation of this Outline should be commended and awarded. The State Council will review and evaluate the implementation of this Outline in due time.